SHÂMAR
TO
SHARIA

SHÂMAR
TO
SHARIA

BIBLICAL ROOTS AND MECHANISMS OF
ISLAMIC RADICALIZATION

J. BARTHOLOMEW WALKER

Quadrakoff Publications Group, LLC
Wilmington, Delaware
USA

Any and all characters appearing that are not in any of the versions
of the Bible are fictional. Any resemblance to any living person is
strictly coincidental.

Cover art is a photograph of an original John Pike watercolor.
Special thanks to Dr. Erich Zion Petrovsky for providing access to
his collection.

Printed in the United States of America.

Many do not understand how it is that Radical Islamic Terrorists could possibly ever come into existence. This is because the process is not understood. It is in fact the very same process encouraged by God when He gave us The Commandments— but here perverted to entirely different ends.

SHÂMAR
TO
SHARIA

Radicalization—a term seemingly incessantly in use today. Bantered back and forth, most assume that this word; or perhaps better stated, the *result* of this *process*; (that of being radicalized; i.e.; that state or condition of being a radical); is well understood by all who participate in these discussions. However; in order to truly understand the result, (that of being radicalized or a radical); one must understand the *process*. And in order to understand that process, one must understand precisely the process for which that particular process, (radicalization), is being proffered as a substitute.

Irrespective of whether or not the result, (radical), is the correct terminology; and thus likewise whether "radicalization" is the correct term for the process; it nevertheless *is*, and *remains* in use. However "radical" is a tricky term, with seemingly mutually exclusive meanings.

If it is assumed that the origin is the Latin "*radix*," then this would indicate the *origin* or *source* of something. But *radiate* generally means to be in or at a place anywhere *except* at the source whence it came. Politically speaking, radicals are rarely called centrists.

"Fundamental," generally refers to a base or foundation. But to be "fundamentalized," and thus resulting in the state of being an "Islamic fundamentalist;" does not seem to sound quite as impressive.

It must be asked precisely how those "radicals," who having become a radical as the direct result of "radicalization;" can be both at the source; and yet at the same time having become "radiated" away from the source?

The answer of course is a matter of perspective. Facts can often be stubborn and unpleasant things. One can argue whether it is a mere preponderance of evidence, clear and convincing evidence, or proof beyond a reasonable doubt; but a fair argument can be made that Islam is or was largely based upon Judaism; but Judaism according to Ishmael, and not Abraham. However; to state that Islam is an *outgrowth* of Judaism would be incorrect. Nevertheless it seems at least arguable that what today is called Judaism; again at least via Ishmael's version of Judaism; provides or provided the basis for what ultimately became Islam. This is a not new concept, as much has been written about it. It is well beyond the scope of this monograph to delve into this theory.

It must also be remembered that in order to truly be anti-Semitic, one must also hate Arabs, as this, (Semitism), is based upon *language* and not *religion*. This is to be distinguished from Zionist, as this is from the Hebrew meaning a *fort* or *stronghold*; i.e.; the State of Israel.

Thus one who is an Islamic fundamentalist, can be characterized as a "radical" meaning being *at* the source, if *Islam* is considered to be the source. However, at the same time he or (she) can be characterized as a radical in the sense of being *away* from the source; if it is understood and so stipulated that the true source of Islam is or was Judaism. It must again be stated that although the *source* of Islam is or may have originally been Judaism, Islam is in no way any type of *outgrowth* of Judaism.

———————————

Practically everyone knows that there are Ten Commandments; written in stone; which we all have been commanded by God to obey. After all, they are called *commandments* and not suggestions. Thus it would seem clear that God has commanded us to obey them.

There are two problems with what here is universally considered to be *epistémē*, or certain knowledge; but what is in fact actually *doxa*, (less than certain), knowledge:

The first; is that in fact there are not and have never been Ten Commandments—at least contained in Exodus 20; but rather there actually are, and have always been only nine. For example: In one attempt to get to ten, it seems that at some point some person or persons, for some reason or reasons; chose to "bust out" the coveting of a wife from the rest of the coveting, thus providing an additional "Commandment."

This likely happened prior to the "modern" era, as it is "wife," and not "spouse" or "partner," that appears in the translations. Others break up the first Commandment into two; with the "no other Gods" and "graven images" parts receiving their very own separate Commandment status and number. Except for perhaps some numerological or Kaballistic concerns, this appears to be a relatively minor point and not particularly germane to the subject at hand—at least at this time.

The second problem; is the purported *requirement to obey* these commandments, which of course is another matter. This is not to say that God does not want us to obey these Commandments; that He would not prefer that we obey these Commandments; or that there are not serious repercussions each and every time these commandments are not obeyed.   Rather, the issue is whether or not He actually told or "commanded" us to obey them.

There is a difference between stating what the laws are; and asking or requiring one to obey them.   The former is *informative* in nature; with the latter being at least arguably *manipulative* in nature.

The Commandments appear for the first time in Exodus 20.

In Exodus 20:6 (KJV)we are told:

> *"And shewing mercy unto thousands of them that love me, and keep my commandments."*[1]

One might reasonably first ask what need there would be for mercy to be shown, (shewn), to those who both love God and also keep, (i.e.; obey), (His) commandments?   Mercy generally refers to not getting what one deserves, (usually in the negative); as opposed to grace, which is getting what one does not deserve, and is usually in the positive.   So then it must be asked that if "keep" means obey, then why would there be any need for any type of mercy to be shown to those "thousands" who are obeying said Commandments? The answer of course: is that by definition there would be no need whatsoever for any such mercy.

The actual Hebrew word translated here as "mercy" is:

"2617 checed; from 2616; *kindness*;..."[2]

"2616 châcad; a prim. root; prop. perh. to
bow (the neck only [comp. 2603] courtesy to
an equal), i.e. to *be kind*;..."[3]

"2603 chânan; a prim. root [comp. 2583];
prop. to *bend* or stoop in kindness to an
inferior; to *favor bestow*..."[4]

A distinction is made here with regard to the roots of
the Hebrew word originally contained in Exodus 20:6
which is translated as "mercy," (*checed* from *châcad*). It
seems that the actual definition of *checed*, is concerned
with showing or providing kindness or courtesy to an
equal; versus the similar word *chânan*, which is
concerned with providing kindness to an *inferior*.

Thus it remains unclear as to why the translators
chose "mercy" as the English translation of *checed*; as
this seems antithetical to its actual meaning. More
precisely; generally in order to show "mercy," one must
necessarily be in a position of superiority with regard to
the potential recipient of any "mercy"—at least with
respect to that particular situation. Here with the use of
checed a position of equality is required.

In Exodus 20:6 it is God who is or was
communicating, so it seems likely He would have
known which Hebrew word to choose to convey His
precise meaning. And He chose the word *checed*, and
not *chânan*. Thus what is clear, in at least in this regard;
is that from this standpoint; (with regard to showing
kindness in *this* context); He (God) considers or

considered us to be equals—else He would have used *chânan*—which He did not.

This may be disturbing to those who attempt to reconcile that which is originally and by design brought into existence in the "image and likeness of God, (H. Sapiens);" with their view of the actual, (real time), current state of the same. This is the inevitable result of conflating the original pure and perfect product, with the current polluted result.

But it seems there is an additional requirement in order to obtain said kindness from the standpoint of being shown kindness as an equal and not as an inferior; as it must be remembered we were told: *"And shewing mercy unto thousands of them that love me, and keep my commandments."*

This can be rephrased as a reversed "if then" declaration: "

> "I, (God), will show you kindness from the standpoint of an equal, if you both love me, *and* also keep my commandments."

The actual Hebrew word translated as "love" is:

> "157 'âhab or 'âhêb; a prim. root: to *have affection* for (sexually or otherwise): - (be-) love (-ed, -ly, -r), like, friend."[5]

Thus the translation as "love," seems reasonably straightforward.

The answer to this "obedience" matter, lies in the actual word which is translated here as "keep."

The actual Hebrew word translated here in Exodus 20:6 as "keep" is:

> "8104: shâmar; A prim. root; prop. to *hedge* about (as with thorns), i.e. *guard*; gen. to *protect*, *attend to*, etc.: - beware, be circumspect, take heed (to self), keep (-er, self), mark, look narrowly, observe, preserve, regard, reserve, save (self), sure, (that lay) wait (for), watch (-man)."[6]

As can easily be seen, the Hebrew word *shâmar*, does not in any way mean obey; but rather to *protect* as though surrounded by a "hedge" of "thorns."

In fact, according to Strong, *shâmar* is not translated as "obey" anywhere in the entire Bible. (See the above provided list of words after the ": -," as these represent all of the Biblical translations of *shâmar*.)

Perhaps God made an error, in that He actually meant to use a word that meant "obey," but was just preoccupied with the ongoing follies of His Chosen Ones at the time.

Or perhaps in fact He actually did use a word that meant "obey," and somehow an error just cropped up in the translation.

Or perhaps Moses actually spoke Hebrew with a serious "Brooklynese" accent, and thus just misunderstood God.

The first of course is impossible. The second is possible; but the problem with this, as well as the latter "perhaps;" is the pesky matter of the "written in stone" part for the content. If God was that serious about not being misunderstood about the rules, He would likely be just as clear about what to do with them.

Much later, Jesus addressed this same issue of love and "obeying" the Commandments.

In John 14:15 (KJV) Jesus tells us:

"If ye love me, keep my commandments."[7]

So it seems clear that Jesus is merely saying: "If you love me, then show it by obeying My commandments."

Or is He?

Here the actual Greek word translated as "keep" is:

"5083 tērĕō; from tĕrŏs (a *watch*; perh. akin to 2334); to *guard* (from *loss* or *injury*, prop. by keeping *the eye* upon..."[8]

Thus the Greek word *tērĕō*, is very synonymic to the aforementioned Hebrew word *shâmar*. And neither *shâmar* nor *tērĕō* is even remotely concerned with obeying the Commandments, or showing *obedience* to anything else.

It is clear that Jesus was not asking for, or even addressing *obedience* either.

In Exodus 20:6, when the Father addressed the matter, He said to shâmar His Commandments—meaning that we should *protect* His Commandments as though to surround them with a hedge of thorns.

Then when Jesus addressed this same matter in John 14:15, the best Greek word for whatever Aramaic word it was that Jesus actually spoke, was the Greek word *tērĕō*—meaning to watch or guard from loss or injury by "keeping the eye upon," His (My) Commandments. In neither case was any type of actual *obedience* to the Commandments sought.

So when God referenced keeping his commandments: "*And shewing mercy unto thousands of them that love me, and keep my commandments*; what is under discussion with regard to His Commandments, is to *protect* (them) as though surrounded by a hedge of thorns. And much later Jesus essentially stated the very same thing.

What possible good are the Commandments if H. Sapiens are not required to *obey* them, but only asked to *guard* them? In truth; at least in this passage; is that He did not even *require* us to guard them; but rather advised us as to what would happen if we loved Him, and if and when we did *shâmar* or guard or protect said Commandments. And why is it that God will show us kindness *as though an (His) equal*, if we merely shâmar His commandments; irrespective of whether or not we actually obey them?

Can it be stated that God does not care if we obey His Commandments? Of course not, as He cares very much whether or not we obey His Commandments—else why would He have provided them. If for no other reason; He cares because of the matter of what is often referred to as *karma*. [This subject is addressed in great detail in the "Second Intermission" of "*MeekRaker Beginnings...*" This mechanism is therein analyzed, and explained on a strictly scientific basis; with the application of the Newtonian laws of F = MA, inertia, and equal and opposite reactions.]

What is much more important to God than H. Sapiens *obeying* His Commandments; is H. Sapiens *choosing* to obey His Commandments. There are two primary things that drive the universe: The first is *free will*; and the second is the aforementioned equal and opposite reactions; i.e.; *karma*.

Many have stated that the entire existence of man consists of nothing more than decision making, or perhaps better stated: "a series of decisions." And of course many have also stated that whatever position(s) a person finds themselves in at any given time, the same is the direct result of all of the decisions one has made up to that point.

Irrespective of whether or not one considers either or both of these beliefs a bit hyperbolic; it nevertheless remains the fact that in the course of one's life, one is forced to make many decisions; including all too often, making the decision to not decide.

But in order to make quality decisions, one requires quality information. This is why with regard to the Commandments; it is *shâmar* that is the concern, and not *obedience*.

What God was saying in Exodus 20:6 is that if we love Him and guard his Commandments as though surrounded by a ""hedge of thorns," he will show kindness to us as though an equal. And later Jesus essentially said the same thing about "guarding." This means to place these Commandments firmly in our intellect; and to protect or guard them; and then to refer back to them when making all decisions. As long as these Commandments are well understood and integrated into the decision making process; said decisions will tend to be the correct ones.

But what about this "as an equal" part?

Genesis 1:28 (KJV) tells us:

> *"And God blessed them,*
> *and God said unto them,*
> *Be fruitful, and multiply,*
> *and replenish the earth,and subdue it:*
> *and have dominion over the fish*
> *of the sea, and over the fowl of the air,*
> *and over every living thing*
> *that moveth upon the earth."*[9]

The actual Hebrew word translated as "replenish" is:

> "4390 mâlê'; or mâlâ' (Esth. 7:5),.; a prim. root, to *fill* or (intrans.) *be full* of, in a wide application (lit. and fig.)..."[10]

It is unclear as to why Esther is referenced here, as mâlê' in Esther 7:5 is translated as "presume" in the KJV.[11]

The actual word translated as "subdue" is:

> "3533 kâbash; a prim. root; to *tread* down; hence neg. to *disregard*; pos. to *conquer*, *subjugate*, *violate*: - bring into bondage, force, keep under, subdue, bring into subjection."[12]

A slight variant of this Hebrew word is seen in current English vernacular, although it is spelled *kibosh.*

The actual Hebrew word translated as "dominion" is:

"7287 râdâh; to *tread* down, i.e. *subjugate*; spec. to *crumble* of: - (come to make to) have dominion, prevail against, reign, (bear, make to) rule, (-r, over), take."[13]

There are two points contained here in Genesis 1:28 worthy of "considerable consideration:"

The *first*; is that it is clear that it is God's will that man have dominion over the earth. God is establishing and instructing His wishes with regard to man's relationship to the earth, *and* all the life forms upon the earth.

God told man to: "*subdue it,*" and "*have dominion.*" Thus this refers to both the earth itself, "*subdue it;*" as well as to "*have dominion*" over all the other various life forms—"*over every living thing that moveth upon the earth.*" [Note that the members of the "audience," appear to be deliberately *excluded*, in terms of man's dominion over any other man, at least at this time.]

In Revelation 7:14 and 19:16 Jesus is referred to as: "King of Kings"[14] and "Lord of Lords."[15]

Given that this appearance is in Revelation, these "kings" or "lords" are generally understood to mean political or quasi-political leaders in the "end times;" of which of course the book of Revelation is actually concerned only in a relative manner. This is usually presented only in the *negative* sense, in that these same kings and lords are, (will be), no match for Jesus; which of course is true.

However; Jesus is also "King of Kings," and "Lord of Lords," in a *positive* sense. This refers to the instructions given to man by the Father in Genesis 1:28. In order for man to have just dominion over the earth and all the life forms upon it; it was necessary for the *Creator* of the earth and all the life forms upon it, who duly had such authority; to grant said authority to man—which is precisely what He did in Genesis 1:28.

Thus from the standpoint of man's relationship to the *earth*; man has an authority similar to God's authority over the universe *as per His will and instructions*. It is for this reason that the kindness He will show us with regard to the Commandments is as an equal, and not an inferior; *checed* and not *chânan*. Thus with regard to the earth, H. Sapiens by design are "little gods." However it must be remembered that there is also the requirement that one must also *love* Him in order to obtain this treatment as an equal.

At this juncture, it would represent gross negligence to not address the "controversial" contents of Psalm 82:6-7, and John 10:34-35.

Psalm 82:6-7 tells us:

> *"I have said, Ye are gods;*
> *and all of you are children of the most High.*
> *But ye shall die like men,*
> *and fall like one of the princes."*[16]

From just these two verses, it is not clear who is speaking; and at first it seems to be God. However;

upon further reading of Psalm 82, it becomes clear that it is likely that it is the author; believed to be Asaph; who is speaking.

If for the purpose of analysis, it can be stipulated that Asaph is in fact a prophet; and is speaking as such here, (on God's behalf); then it is clear that in this passage, H. Sapiens are considered to be described as (little) "gods."

The actual Hebrew word translated here as "gods" is:

> "430 'ĕlôhîym; plur. of 433; *gods* in the ordinary sense; but spec. used (in the plur. thus, esp. with the art.) of the supreme *God*; occasionally applied by way of deference to *magistrates*; and sometimes as a superlative: - angels, x exceeding, God (gods) (-dess, -ly), x (very) great, judges, x mighty.[17]

This statement in Psalms 82:6 is considered to be highly controversial, as many are uncomfortable with the notion that H. Sapiens are in any way to be considered "gods."

Since Psalm 82 is generally considered to be a rebuke of unjust judges, many prefer to believe that the "occasionally applied by way of deference to *magistrates*" translation should apply. This then supplants "gods" with "judges." This then solves their problem of H. Sapiens being declared in any way "gods."

However it must be noted that this is the very same Hebrew word for God, ('ĕlôhîym); that appears in Exodus 20:2 where God Himself states:

"I am the LORD thy God ('ĕlôhîym), which
have brought thee out of the land of Egypt,
out of the house of bondage."[18]

Others; those who accept "gods" as the correct translation here; then rely on Psalm 82 verse 7 to disprove H. Sapiens being any type of "god," as again it states:

"But ye shall die like men,
and fall like one of the princes."[19]

This is where the context; i.e.; the audience of corrupt judges, becomes significant. Rather than disproving that *'ĕlôhîym* actually means "gods;" this is instead a statement of what will *become* of that which originally and by design were 'ĕlôhîym or "gods," because of their subsequent behaviors.

And then John 10:34-35 tells us:

"Jesus answered them,
Is it not written in your law,
I said, Ye are gods?
If he called them gods,
unto whom the word of God came,
and the scripture cannot be broken;"[20]

The actual Greek word translated here as "gods" in "Ye are gods" is:

"2316 thĕŏs; of uncert. affin.; a *deity*, espec. (with 3588) the supreme *Divinity*; fig. a *magistrate*; by Heb. *very*: - x exceeding, God, god [-ly, -ward].[21]

Here again is the *figurative* use for a magistrate.

According to Strong, this very same word, (thĕŏs), appears again in the included phrase: "*word of God.*"[22]

Thus; the same word used to describe God in "*word of God,*" is used to describe H. Sapiens in the preceding "*Ye (H. Sapiens) are gods.*"

As an aside, there is an interesting use of the first person by Jesus asking about what He "said," as contained in their written "law." Psalms is considered to have been written many centuries prior to Jesus' birth.

And *secondly*; there is that inescapable point which it seems is almost universally overlooked. Most consider the creation of the earth to be a process, with Genesis 1:2 et. seq. simply representing or describing a part or a stage of this creation process. The "without form, void, and dark" therefore being considered a *transitional* state, ultimately resulting in the creation of the final product: earth.

Many or most consider the conditions and events which appear after Genesis 1:1, as a mere *recapitulation* of events occurring in Genesis 1:1—which they are not. This is despite the fact that Genesis 1:1 ends with the word earth, and Genesis 1:2 begins with earth, right after the "pickup notes." Litigating this error is beyond the scope of this monograph. However, this extremely significant widespread error is rectified in great referenced detail in the initial chapters of "*MeekRaker Beginnings...*"

If it were true that "without form, void, and dark" were merely transitional states in the process of the creation of the earth; there then would be one inescapable fact. The same being: that according to God's instructions as contained in Genesis 1:28; God necessarily must have created a final product for man, (the earth), that required in English; "putting the kibosh on;" or in Hebrew; *kâbash*(ing). This is certain because God Himself instructed man to "kâbash; a prim. root; to *tread* down; hence neg. to *disregard*; pos. to *conquer, subjugate, violate*: - bring into bondage, force, keep under, subdue, bring into subjection" the earth—arguably in order to be able to live on it. As though somehow God was incapable of creating an earth that did not require *kâbash*(ing).

One alternative explanation would be that although God *could* have created a world where *kâbash*(ing) was not necessary, He nevertheless chose not to. The more this possible explanation is pondered, the more absurd any such contention becomes.

The truth; is that the end of Genesis 1:1 represents a statement of completion; of the final product; of the creation of the earth—which is exactly what is stated.

Genesis 1:2 onward is not any type of "flashback" to some point in time in the middle of Genesis 1:1; but rather describes the condition of the earth at some unspecified point in time after time *after* its creation or completion. Although most of the more popular translations/versions do not contain this, the *Interlinear Bible* includes "she became," prior to the subsequent description of "without form, void, and dark" condition of the earth.[23]

It is clear in literal reading of Genesis, that God subsequently intervened in the altered condition of the originally completed earth; but intervened only to a certain point—which is why it was that man was *created*, and then instructed by God to subdue or *kâbash* the earth in Genesis 1:28. This was not because God *could* not do it, but rather because He *would* not do it. This was the result of the allocation of His *authority*, and had nothing to do with His *capabilities*.

The only *"primum movens"* or prime mover is God. God is the only entity that exists without a cause. This is a major problem for science regarding the cause of the origin of the universe. Genesis 1:1 is merely a description of the result of the "Big Bang," with the responsible party, (cause), stated therein. Any and all other entities except God are either results or causes; and are at the same time both. When the earth *became* without form, void and dark; this was a result that required a cause; and this cause clearly was not God.

———————

Without getting into too much detail, it is clear that there exists an entity that is active in opposing the will of God. Although there seems to be a plethora of *doxa* about this entity; there is a paucity of *epistéme*.

What is known, is that this entity was "thrown down" to the earth; likely at some time between Genesis 1:1 and Genesis 1:2. (For much greater detail on this, see: "*Ostium Ab Inferno—The Opening From Hell*") What is also known is that man is to have dominion over "all the life forms upon the earth." This includes that which was "thrown down."

What is not known is the actual origin of this opposition entity. Any serious and logical contemplation of the actual origin of this opposing entity necessarily leaves one in a bit of a conundrum, and thus is beyond the scope of this monograph. Although the *results* of the infection are described; neither the original *source*, (possible tautology noted), nor the *vector* is known.

What is also important and germane here, is that in keeping with this; i.e.; in the consideration of *shâmar* (H), or *tērĕō* (G); there is a clear unmistakable implication—arguably a requirement—of or for something to *guard* these Commandments *from*.

Said entity—by all of its various names, is in the overall business of opposing the will of God in the general sense; and violently opposed to *man* carrying out the will of God in the specific. Said "adversary" to God, and "enemy" to man, basically has two choices:

The first; is to be involved on a "case by case" basis in interfering with each and every decision being made by those in the "*image and likeness*" of God; if and when said decision would be in furtherance of the will of God. The enemy can "go to lunch," if the decision appears to be against the will of God, as it is pleased with this. However this "case by case," is a very messy and very "time consuming" process, requiring many "demon-hours" of effort. It will do this seemingly incessantly, but this is a grossly inefficient process.

The *second* method; and the one that is much more efficient for it, (the enemy or adversary); is for it to carefully attack that which is utilized as the principles by which one makes decisions. It is against this very attack that God wishes us to *shâmar* or *tērĕō*, that which is contained in His Commandments.

For example: If one fully understands: "Thou shall not steal," and incorporates this in the decision making process; then usually one is not likely to take that which rightfully belongs to another. In order for the enemy to win, it then has to wage a battle each and every time the opportunity for theft arises.

If however, it can successfully attack this: "Thou shall not steal" principle, by getting through that protective hedge of thorns, (via either inadequate *shâmar*, or overwhelming force); and then supplant this with something such as: "Stealing is okay, as long as you do not get caught;" then most or all future battles regarding stealing itself suddenly become unnecessary.

The target or victim of this attack will now *shâmar* this new "principle;" and behave in a manner consistent with this "new rule." Going forward; it no longer will be the issue of *stealing* being a wrongdoing to be avoided; but rather the issue of *getting caught* being the wrongdoing to be avoided, which then guides the behavior. So although *stealing* was once an abomination; it has now become acceptable, with only the prospect of *getting caught* now being that which is abominable.

One only need look at automobiles to see the regression of the quality of that which is *shâmar*(ed) currently in the United States. As late as the early 1960's, automobile ignition switches had a "lock," and an "off" position. This "off" position was a means by which when the engine was shut off and the key was removed, the vehicle could still be started and driven without the key—by design. Today, anti-theft devices are extremely complicated and complex. This was not done because of any overall decrease in the incidence of auto theft.

That which is *shâmar*(ed) by H. Sapiens in the US has changed dramatically; shifting from principled rules, to self-centered thinking. This was not only predictable, but done by design by those in power whose goals are antithetical to the will of God—the same being His primary desire for the *free will* of man. Once this is understood, many seemingly inexplicable actions; particularly by political leaders; begin to make perfect sense.

Often cited as justification, this concept of "separation of church and state;" which appears nowhere in the US constitution; *should* be utilized to prevent a theocracy, and not to justify serious infringements on the 1st Amendment to the US Constitution. "Someone might be offended," grossly falls far short of a "clear and present danger," or any similar subsequent test. In fact it was primarily for religious and political expression that the 1st Amendment was ratified.

If there is any legitimate use for "separation of church and state" rule; this should be utilized to prevent the government from religious proselytizing, not to be used to justify 1st Amendment restrictions on US citizens, simply because of a money trail purportedly providing the government with jurisdiction—i.e.; the *authority*, but not the *right*.

To the extent that God and His rules for behavior can be removed, made inaccessible, or determined to be "uncool;" then His rules are necessarily then supplanted by man's rules, which over millennia simply did not work. Clearly one cannot *shâmar* what one has never read or understood. This is not an unintended consequence, but rather the main objective of those who are making access to God's word as difficult as possible.

The inevitable result of this, is a government that can, (now must), become ever increasingly involved with regulating what H. Sapiens *can* do, because what H. Sapiens *will* do has changed so dramatically. This change is the direct result of deliberately and with malice, making God's rules as inaccessible as possible. Automobile ignition switches are merely one result or symptom.

What is even more dangerous; is that the current, (modern), state of behavior of H. Sapiens; is generally viewed as an *end* of a process, and not merely a snapshot of a *stage* in a process. Meaning; that unless something dramatically changes, behavior will continue to degenerate until there is little to no freedom left. But then again, that is and always was the intention of those; who unlike God; find the free will of man not only repulsive, but often times abominable. It is far better to be in quicksand, and know one is in quicksand; than it is to be in the very same quicksand, and not even realize it.

There are two main differences between so called radicalization of Islamic terrorists, and what is happening in the US today.

In the so called radicalization of Islamic terrorists, whatever the "recruit" may have previously *shâmar*(ed), is supplanted by what someone said someone else said, about what someone said someone else said. . ., ad nauseum; about what someone may have written circa 700AD. The "recruit" is rapidly forced to *shâmar* what he/she is told to *shâmar*, based upon said hearsay, from this "original" source.

And although said "original" source, "originally" was Judaism, (via Abraham); this newer "original" source, Judaism, (via Ishmael); is at a minimum highly questionable. But it is nevertheless God and His purported will, which provides the motive for Islamic "radicalization;" and the subsequent actions of the resultant Islamic radical.

The ultimate determination of success of the "radicalized," is that individual working what was previously a "measure of faith;" but now by requiring all others to obey what he was recently commanded and chose to *shâmar*. Should anyone, (infidel), choose to *shâmar* what he or they believe God said to *shâmar*; and not what the "radical" now commands them to *shâmar*, they simply are killed. And said terrorist is not only willing to die him or herself as a consequence of the furtherance of this process of killing what he now considers infidels; but welcomes the opportunity, as he has also been told and now considers his death in killing others as an honor.

Islamic terrorists actually believe that they both *know* and are zealously *obeying* the will of God. As insane as this, (the Islamic terrorists'), interpretation of the will of God may be, this nevertheless remains manipulation by *commission* with respect to God; as all of this is done in what is believed to be in furtherance of the same.

It also seems clear that in Islam, there is this extreme misunderstanding regarding the coming of Messiah. It is difficult to determine with any degree of precision the nature of this misunderstanding. It seems that the Islamic Mahdi is analogous to Judeo/Christian Messiah. Whether it is believed that the 12th Imam is the Mahdi, or Islam's Messiah; or will merely *accompany* the Messiah, is difficult to determine. Likewise it is difficult to determine precisely who it is that may have been hidden, (occultation), for perhaps some 1200 years.

Although conflated by many in Christianity and Judaism, the Bible references to Messiah as the "fuller's soap," and the "great and dreadful day" of the Lord;" are references to two different events. The former refers to the first coming, and the latter to the second coming of Messiah.

A fair argument can be made that in Islam, it is not believed that the first coming, (for salvation and redemption), has yet happened; as is also the case with Judaism. Or perhaps better phrased; that which is required for salvation has not yet occurred, irrespective of who it is that may currently be involved in any "occultation." If it can be so stipulated that this is *incorrect*—meaning that when Messiah comes it will be the *second* time, then some degree of sense can be made out of this.

Mainstream Christianity believes that the first coming has already occurred, and there will be a period of tribulation prior to the *second* coming of Jesus. Many believe that this will be preceded by the rapture, where current believers will be taken up to heaven *in corpus*. If this is so, this will result in only non-believers being left on the earth at that juncture. If this, (rapture), is not so; both believers and non-believers will experience the tribulation.

Either way, there is to be a period of tribulation on earth; the purpose being for a final opportunity to accept Messiah, and thus be "saved." During this time, "believers" will be persecuted and killed by the enemy of God. At some point; (the end of the tribulation); there will be the return of Jesus.

"Anti-Christ" or not, in Christianity it is the *enemy* who is responsible for persecution of believers; as well as providing the ensuing chaos which Jesus ultimately resolves.

In "radical" Islam, it seems things are a bit backwards. The "radicals" are killing *non-believers*, (by their standards); leaving only believers; (again by their standards). Thus by their standards, to the extent they succeed; only Islamic "believers" will be left at the Christian second coming, or it seems what may be the Islamic *only* coming.

Since Islam does not seem to be particularly big on the idea of reincarnation, those who do not accept radical Islam are knowingly; (according to radical Islam); being sent to eternal damnation. This is not by their own choice to not believe in Messiah; but rather by the *deliberate* choices of those very same Islamic "radicals" who kill them.

The purported purpose of the Tribulation, is to provide such overwhelming evidence for choosing to accept Messiah; that one can make no other *logical* decision, other than to *choose* to accept Messiah.

The purpose of Islamic "radicals," is by the threat of immediate physical death, to force belief in Islam; or to forever be denied the option of salvation; (according to the killers understanding).

It must be asked which belief it is that represents a loving and just God?

The ongoing degeneration of behavior of H. Sapiens in the US, is a bit different. Here there are and have been "progressive," and thus long term attempts to; unlike the terrorists; *remove* the entire concept of God; and let behavior be determined by whatever it is that one "chooses" to *shâmar*; that is: *as long as it is always the case that God's rules are not considered.* This is the same reason why it is a crime in many Muslim countries to possess, study, or preach the Bible?

It must be remembered that *progressivism*, (in the political context), is not a political ideology; but rather is a tactic or strategy, depending upon its use.

To characterize one's self as a "progressive" *politically*, merely means that one believes in placing the frog in a pot of cold water and placing the pot on the stove; rather than placing the frog in boiling water; because the frog then could and likely would simply jump out.

The enemy is and has been an expert at this type of progressivism. In fact it can be reasonably argued that he (it) invented it.

In the US, God's rules are, and have for quite some time, been progressively removed; so that they are not readily available for consideration when making choices. Instead of concrete, (written in stone), rules for behavior; what one *shâmar*(s) has become an ongoing "learning" process, and is subject to changes and modifications.

This is; in contradistinction to the terrorists; manipulation by *omission* with respect to God.

Long term karmic, (equal and opposite reactions), are the basis for God's rules. But man's rules today are largely based upon the short term, particularly *feelings*; (as commonly defined). Things that make one "feel good," are now acceptable; and things that make one feel bad; or sometimes make or may make another feel bad, are not. Giving a student the failing grade that they earned, is frowned upon because of how it could make the student *feel*. What is the likelihood of long term success, when failure is rewarded in the short term and shortsighted concern for feelings?

This is a supplanting of the objective with the subjective. Meaning; that the rules that God stated are based upon the objective—the quantity and quality of that which is or will be the actual result of one's choices. But these supplanting factors are largely not based upon what will *actually* happen, but rather based largely upon what is *believed* will happen to *me*.

This then concomitantly results in the supplanting of actuality with reality. Actuality being here defined as that which "actually" exists; as opposed as to reality being that which is perceived and *believed* to exist. When the appropriate reality, (that which is consistent with actuality); ultimately collides with subjective and self-centered reality, things become anything but boring.

God's will for the free will of man is both an absolute and non-absolute. It is an absolute in the sense of man being completely free to make whatever choice(s) he wishes. And it is also an absolute, in that whatever is sown will ultimately be reaped.

However God's will for man's free will is also a non-absolute, in that interfering with another's free will provides the boundary. Thus free will, as is the case with many things, must be kept in balance.

1 Corinthians 8:9 (KJV) tells us:

> *"But take heed lest by any means this liberty of yours become a stumbling block to them that are weak."*[24]

This "subjectivation," can be seen with the longstanding, but seemingly now obsolete, "clear and present danger et seq.," tests for infringing upon one's free speech. There was a time where imminent actual harm to another was required, (interference to another's will to remain unharmed), before free speech could be infringed.

This has changed dramatically. There is an ongoing war about infringing upon free speech in an attempt to supplant "clear and present," with "may or might;" and supplanting "danger," with "hurt the feelings" of someone in disagreement with these words. This is extremely dangerous; and clearly inconsistent with both the US Constitution, and the will of God.

Another difference between so called radicalization and progressivism is the time factor. "Radicalization" is accomplished in a relatively short period of time.

Political progressivism however, has been at work for well over a century, (see Woodrow Wilson). Said progressivism is at this time not quite eugenics, as that became taboo because of adherents such as Adolph Hitler. It is currently much more about gradually obtaining *control* than destruction—at least for now. Given that the US was originally based upon free will and Judeo-Christian principles, slow and methodical changes are required by the "progressives"—lest the frog jump out. [See: *"Statists Saving One"*]

The result of Islamic Radicalism and concomitant "sharia law;" is the predictable, (and deliberate), effect of a cause. That cause being the supplanting of that which God desires us to *shâmar*, with something contrary to the concept of free will entirely. It must be noted that much of sharia is merely *derived*.

Thus; quite unlike the actual Judeo-Christian Commandments; sharia is not even proffered to be the literal Word of God. Instead it is proffered as "what He really meant" (according to me); as opposed to *what He actually said*.

God can never have it both ways, and neither can the Islamists. Unfortunately; this derivation is not unique to Islam. It could reasonably be argued that the Muslim Hadith, the Jewish Talmud, and various Christian "pronunciamentos" all have this "derivation" issue in common.

But what is to be done about it?

As most know; whether or not it is known that it is known; initially, the attacks of the enemy are oppressive. This oppression is similar to an infestation or *ectoparisitosis*.

For example: attacks upon the person who has chosen to *shâmar*: "Thou shalt not steal;" are attacks that are situation specific, (oppressive); attacks from *without*. ("Go ahead and take it, no one is looking.") And although some may succeed "short term;" they generally do not succeed long term. This is because these attacks have little long term effect upon what it is that *guides* the behavior. There is an imbalance created between the thoughts ideas and suggestions comprising the attack; and that which is protected or guarded, ("Thou shalt not steal," via *shâmar*.

The attack, (TIS attack; thoughts, ideas and suggestions), may succeed either totally or partially; but there nevertheless remains the unbalanced force created by the imbalance between the suggested action, (the attack), or the action itself; and that which is guarded or protected. And this unbalanced force must eventually be balanced. Said imbalance can be balanced by outright rejection. Here the hand grenade is quickly hurled back at the attacker: "Here if you like it so much; and if it is such a good idea, you take it."

However; to the extent that the attack succeeds, there is created an imbalance which must be subjectively balanced. In the use of progressive techniques, (including and most especially political progressivism); the idea is to balance this imbalance by a change, even if only a slight change, in that which is *shâmar*(ed).

"It was only a dollar, so it is fine;" or "It was only a white lie." Here the definition of stealing or lying, is changed from an absolute to a relative. Initially, taking the *property of*, or the *truth from*, another was wrong; but now it becomes relative, in that below a certain threshold, it is not now considered actually stealing or lying. The purpose of the next attack of course, will be to again raise the threshold. Eventually one finds themselves robbing banks, and does not even know how they got there.

These *subjective* imbalances, are to be distinguished from the *objective* karmic or "equal and opposite reaction" imbalances, created by any and all actions.

However; for a variety of reasons beyond the scope of this monograph; this oppressive and *infestation* like ectoparasitosis, can "progress," to possessive and *infection* like endoparasitosis.

This can be on one area, or many areas. This can be constant or intermittent. This can be constant in one area for a time, and absent in another. This variation is determined not as much by the intensity of the attack, but rather largely by the resistance of the host. Infectious disease operates in a similar manner. Any time the external invasive forces overcome the internal resistive forces, "dis-ease" is the result. This is the rule in both the material and immaterial realms.

To suggest that the Islamic terrorists represent the *most* heinous result of the supplanting of that which should be "*shâmar*(ed)" with that which is not of God; would likely reveal an inexcusable ignorance of history. Nevertheless, it would be both naive and dangerous, to not recognize the presence of this level of evil now present in the world.

It seems that there are only two ways in which this menace can be remedied:

The first would be to find a means by which to "un*shâmar*" that which these individuals have chosen to shâmar. However there are some problems associated with this approach:

> 1) Unless these terrorists can be taught of their own free will to *choose* to remove that which they currently shâmar, (by their own previous choosing); this would then be *manipulative* in nature. Thus even though the techniques

involved would in no way resemble the terrorist techniques, at the root nevertheless remains manipulation—which would be just as much against the will of God as the manipulation by the terrorists or anyone else.

2) Even if this approach were possible, the free will of the *victims* of the remaining or unconverted, (still radicalized), terrorists; would continue to be under attack by terrorists during the process. This would then mean that the free will and God given rights of the terrorists; who after all *are* the active and menacing parties; would be placed higher than the rights of these innocent victims who just want to exercise *their* free will and God given rights.

3) In terms of raw numbers, the actual number of "conversion" of current terrorists, would have to exceed the number of those who are being "radicalized" or "recruited." The positive or negative "delta" or difference would then be the measure of success or failure. With the number of Muslims currently in the world today, even a very small percentage as a "recruitment rate" represents a rather large number—an amount which would likely increase as news of mass (re)conversions spread.

Unfortunately; the only alternative at this time seems to be complete and total destruction of each and every Islamic terrorist on a consistent and ongoing basis.

1 Samuel 15:18:

> *"And the LORD sent thee on a journey,*
> *and said, Go and utterly destroy the sinners*
> *the Amalekites, and fight against*
> *them until they be consumed."*[25]

> *Excessive free will easily*
> *becomes manipulation.*
> —*Emma B. Quadrakoff*

J. Bartholomew Walker

ABOUT THE MEEKRAKER SERIES

Whathat on earth is a MeekRaker?
This word can be broken down into two parts "Meek" and "Raker." Capital letters were used in order to minimize any mispronunciations such as Mee-kraker; but the "etymology" is actually the fusion of these two words.

What is meek? And who in their right mind would ever want to be meek? Courage, strength, and bravery are characteristics that are generally considered desirable; but meek? No thanks. Unfortunately, the meaning of this word has been distorted over time to include things such as timidity, or shyness; weakness, or cowardice, but this is not; or rather should not be so.

Chambers states:

> "meek adj. Probably before 1200 meok gentle, humble, in Ancrene Riwle; later mec (probably about 1200, in the *The Ormlum*);

borrowed from a Scandanavian source (Compare Old Icelandic mjukr soft pliant gentle....")[AT-1]

These origins seem to be adjectival in nature, and describe a condition of humility or softness. Thus a meek person, by these definitions would indicate a humble or soft person. The opposite of this would then be a person who is prideful or hard.

Humble vs. prideful is an easy one. Who would want to be prideful? The Bible is replete with warnings about pride; and it was pride that started all of the messes to begin with. Pride may make one "feel good" for a short period of time, but as previously referenced; the Bible is quite clear that on that path there lies destruction.

But what does the Bible actually have to say about being a meek person?

- It tells us that the meek shall (*not will or might*) inherit the earth.[AT-2]
- It further tells us that the meek will be guided in judgment will be taught His way.[AT-3]
- The meek will be lifted up by the Lord, and He will cast the wicked down to the ground.[AT-4]
- He will save all the meek of the earth.[AT-5]

And what about the Bible's statements regarding being "hard?"

- "For their heart was hardened."[AT-6] "Have ye your heart yet hardened?"[AT-7]
- "... their eyes and hardened their heart."[AT-8]
- "But they and our fathers dealt proudly, and hardened their necks, and hearkened not to thy commandments, and refused to obey, neither were mindful of thy wonders that thou didst among them; but hardened their necks, and in their rebellion..."[AT-9]
- "Happy is the man that feareth always: But he that hardeneth his heart shall fall into mischief."[AT-10]
- "He that being often reproved hardeneth his neck, shall suddenly be destroyed, and that without remedy."[AT-11]

The actual word in all of these citations which is translated as hard is:

"4456 poroo (a kind of stone); to *petrify*, i.e. (fig.) to *indurate* (*render stupid* or *callous*): - blind, harden.[AT-12]

With respect to hard, there is a clear Scriptural relationship between the same and disobedience; not being "mindful" of God performing wonders in one's life, rebellious, falling into "mischief," and being "destroyed," "without remedy."

In addition, by the very definition of the original word, one who is "hard" is also stupid callous and blind. (If a physical heart were actually to turn into stone, you are just dead; so surely that definition does not apply in this context or usage.)

Thus, meek or soft; that being the opposite of hard; would tend to be obedient, be mindful of God performing wonders, not rebellious, not falling into mischief, and not destroyed. Furthermore, one would not be "stupid," "callous" or "blind."

The use of the term meek as "soft," also implies *teachable*.

Hardhead: will not change mind. Hardhearted: will not change heart. Hard necked: junction between head and heart is hard, and will not permit mental change to be transmitted to change the heart.

If it is firmly established that the term "revelation" has the prerequisite of being *the* truth; when confronted with potential revelation; it has been the authors' experiences that hard persons; specifically those of the head, neck, and heart variety; will generally behave according to the "Three A's:"

> A_1 is *anger*. This is the first response. This anger is not so much because there is a remote chance that they may be wrong, but rather when it is somewhat clear that they *are* wrong. This would be best illustrated as a line on a graph rising from left to right; with the level of anger represented by the vertical axis, and time represented by the horizontal axis.
>
> A_2 is *argument*. This generally begins with emotionally (anger) driven arguments. As

the arguments begin to fail, the level and usually the slope of A_1 will increase. When all possible arguments, logical, relevant or otherwise have been proffered, the original arguments will then return. This would be best illustrated as a circle under the rising anger line referenced above. Often, what is just under the skin, (which is generally the reason for the pride and subsequent anger) will pop its "head" out; revealing things previously unknown about this individual.

A_3 is *absconding*. When all of the arguments and the repetition thereof have unquestionably failed, the hard person will generally abscond; or run away. This may be represented by actual physical separation, changing the subject or in some other manner. This could be perceived as the disappearance of the anger line, but is only subjective; as the true level of anger then becomes somewhat hidden.

Contrarily, the *meek* will weigh the value of any purported revelation; and then decide precisely what it is that merits their belief. Sincere questioning and even some arguments will be presented; but here not with the primary purpose of proving that they, the inquirer, is correct; but rather to understand precisely what it is that this revelation represents; knowing that if it in fact does represent revelation, then this will be to their benefit. A logical decision will then be made with respect to what constitutes the truth.

The primary basis for the actions of a "hard-head," is *emotional.* The primary basis for the actions of the meek; although perhaps including some emotional factors; (i.e. passion); is largely *intellectual.*

In a sense, the purpose of a rake is to separate the soft from the hard. The Bible refers to separating the wheat from the chaff, the silver from the dross; hence the origin of "*MeekRaker*". Meek or hard is not so much determined by what one believes; but rather by the *process* involved in making these determinations.

Bibliography

1. *The Holy Bible, KJV* Exodus 20:6,
   kingjamesbibleonline.org, retrieved 7 March 2016
2. Strong, James. *Strong's Exhaustive Concordance of the
   Bible.* © 1890 James Strong, Madison, NJ p. 41(Hebrew)
3. Strong, James. *Strong's Exhaustive Concordance of the
   Bible.* © 1890 James Strong, Madison, NJ p. 41(Hebrew)
4. Strong, James. *Strong's Exhaustive Concordance of the
   Bible.* © 1890 James Strong, Madison, NJ p. 41(Hebrew)
5. Strong, James. *Strong's Exhaustive Concordance of the
   Bible.* © 1890 James Strong, Madison, NJ p. 9(Hebrew)
6. Strong, James. *Strong's Exhaustive Concordance of the
   Bible.* © 1890 James Strong, Madison, NJ p. 118(Hebrew)
7. *The Holy Bible, KJV* John 14:15, *kingjamesbibleonline.org,*
   retrieved 7 March 2016
8. Strong, James. *Strong's Exhaustive Concordance of the
   Bible.* © 1890 James Strong, Madison, NJ p. 71(Greek)
9. *The Holy Bible, KJV* Genesis 1:28,
   kingjamesbibleonline.org, retrieved 7 March 2016

10. Strong, James. *Strong's Exhaustive Concordance of the Bible.* ©   1890 James Strong, Madison, NJ p. 66(Hebrew)

11. *The Holy Bible, KJV* Esther 7:5, *kingjamesbibleonline.org*, retrieved 7 March 2016

12. Strong, James. *Strong's Exhaustive Concordance of the Bible.* © 1890 James Strong, Madison, NJ p. 54(Hebrew)

13. Strong, James. *Strong's Exhaustive Concordance of the Bible.* © 1890 James Strong, Madison, NJ p. 107(Hebrew)

14. *The Holy Bible, KJV* Revelation 7:14, *kingjamesbibleonline.org*, retrieved 7 March 2016

15. *The Holy Bible, KJV* Revelation 19:16, *kingjamesbibleonline.org*, retrieved 7 March 2016

16. *The Holy Bible, KJV* Psalm 82:6-7, *kingjamesbibleonline.org*, retrieved 7 March 2016

17. Strong, James. *Strong's Exhaustive Concordance of the Bible.* © 1890 James Strong, Madison, NJ p. 12(Hebrew)

18. *The Holy Bible, KJV* Exodus 20:2, *kingjamesbibleonline.org*, retrieved 7 March 2016

19. *The Holy Bible, KJV* Psalm 82:7, *kingjamesbibleonline.org*, retrieved 7 March 2016

20. *The Holy Bible, KJV* John 10:34-35, *kingjamesbibleonline.org*, retrieved 7 March 2016

21. Strong, James. *Strong's Exhaustive Concordance of the Bible.* © 1890 James Strong, Madison, NJ p. 36(Greek)

22. Strong, James. *Strong's Exhaustive Concordance of the Bible.* © 1890 James Strong, Madison, NJ p. 407

23. *Interlinear Bible Hebrew Greek English, 1 Volume Edition.* © 1976, 1977, 1978, 1979, 1980, 1981, 1984. Second Edition, © 1986 Jay P. Green, Sr., Hendrickson Publishers (Genesis 1:2)

24. *The Holy Bible, KJV* 1st Corinthians 8:9,
   kingjamesbibleonline.org, retrieved 7 March 2016
25. *The Holy Bible, KJV* 1st Samuel 15:18,
   kingjamesbibleonline.org, retrieved 7 March 2016

About the MeekRaker Series Title

AT1 *Chambers Dictionary of Etymology*. Copyright © 1988
   The H. W. Wilson Company, New York, NY p.648
AT2 *www.kingjamesbibleonline.org* (KJV) (Matt.5:5)
   retrieved June 2011
AT3 *www.kingjamesbibleonline.org* (KJV) (Ps. 25:9)
   retrieved June 2011
AT4 *www.kingjamesbibleonline.org* (KJV) (Ps. 147:6)
   retrieved June 2011
AT5 *www.kingjamesbibleonline.org* (KJV) (Ps. 76:9)
   retrieved June 2011
AT6 *www.kingjamesbibleonline.org* (KJV) (Mark 6:52)
   retrieved June 2011
AT7 *www.kingjamesbibleonline.org* (KJV) (Mark 8:17)
   retrieved June 2011

AT8 *www.kingjamesbibleonline.org* (KJV) (John 12:40) retrieved June 2011

AT9 *www.kingjamesbibleonline.org* (KJV) (Neh. 9:16) retrieved June 2011

AT10 *www.kingjamesbibleonline.org* (KJV) (Prov. 28:14) retrieved June 2011

AT11 *www.kingjamesbibleonline.org* (KJV) (Prov. 29:1) retrieved June 2011

AT12 Strong, James. *Strong's Exhaustive Concordance of the Bible.* © 1890 James Strong, Madison, NJ p. 63 (Greek)

Other Fine QPG Publications:

MEEKRAKER BEGINNINGS...

From the inside flap of *"MeekRaker Beginnings..."*

"The primary purpose of this tome, is the reconciliation of the word of God with science; and to do so in such a manner as to be rendered inarguable by any rational mind. As stated in the Preface: "One must choose between being a "man of science" or a believer," because they are generally considered to be mutually exclusive. If one agrees that words mean things, then an unbiased fair read of God's Word presents no such paradox. But one must read what God actually said, not merely what one thinks He said, what one was told He said, what one wished He said, or would rather He had said."

Wisdom Essentials—*The Pentalogy*

"That Which is Difficult If Not Impossible to Find Anywhere Else—All In One Place!"

But there are many other effects for which no material cause can be found. In *"Donald Trump*

Candidacy According to Matthew?" his meteoric rise and seeming inability to fail are explained according to Biblical principles. Since this is a non-political work, his success was not actually prophesied, but no other conclusion could possibly have been drawn—*and this was published long before he was even nominated.*

In *"SHÂMAR TO SHARIA,"* the process of radical indoctrination is analyzed, and is shown to be a perversion of that very same thing God instructed man to do with the Commandments, and how this is not in any way limited to terrorists.

"It's Not Just A Theory" examines the relationship between behavior and longevity according to both science and the Scriptures; and "according to both" also includes major consistencies.

"Calvary's Hidden Truths" reveals many unknown facts about what actually occurred at that time.

"Inevitable Balance" scientifically and Biblically explains that which is often observed but rarely understood: Why "What Goes Around Comes Around;" AKA *karma,* or the "law of compensation."

STATISTS SAVING ONE

"The Malignant Sophistry of
Rights Removal by the Far Left"

"...under the umbrella of "liberals" or "liberalism;" (as used today); there are actually two separate and distinct groups:

"True liberals believe very much in what they promulgate. They are truly concerned with the welfare of citizens, and they believe in policies that will benefit the same—at least in their view. There are neither nefarious purposes, nor any intellectual dishonesty. Their objective is to improve the quality of life (and longevity), for as many people as possible.

"...Conservatives and liberals can often agree on the ends; but vastly disagree on the means. Giving a hungry person a fish is kind; but to conservatives, teaching him how to fish seems to be a better long term solution. It is not that conservatives object to the temporary giving of the fish; but rather they object to not teaching him how to fish.

"True liberals believe in the dignity of man; and promulgate policies in furtherance of this belief.
"Statists; the other group usually and often erroneously grouped under the "liberal" umbrella; are another matter. It is because of agreements with liberal policy that they are usually grouped under this liberal umbrella;

but their motivations, purposes and beliefs are entirely different—arguably antithetical—to true liberalism."

OSTIUM AB INFERNO
[*The Opening From Hell*]

"The Original Monograph - According to the Father, The Christ Son and The Holy Ghost"

- What is "hell"? Why is there a hell?
- What openings from "hell" exist?
- What is the truth about "Abraham's Bosom?" And how does this or do these affect man?

- What are angels?
- Are angels named such because of structure or function?
- Is it true that one third were banished to hell? If true why, and when did this all happen?

Much of that which is fanciful has been written about these questions. But the answers should not be sought from that which is the product of men's imaginations—albeit these may provide interesting reading. Rather; the answers should be sought from, and always remain: "according to The Father, The Christ Son, and The Holy Ghost." (Written in English.)

REINCARNATION —A REASONABLE INQUIRY

"Often times it is emotion(s) and not facts that determine what it is that is believed to be 'in fact so.'" —p.6

"When truth and perceived practicality conflict; unfortunately it is truth that often becomes the sacrificial lamb." —p.91

"He that answereth a matter before he heareth it, it is folly and shame unto him."

—Proverbs 18:13 (KJV)

Some say reincarnation is a fact, and cite the Bible as the unimpeachable source regarding this matter.

Others say reincarnation is fiction, and cite the Bible as the unimpeachable source regarding this very same matter.

One of these groups is about to be shocked.

QPG Publications are available
wherever you buy fine books.

For a full list of QPG publications,
visit us at MeekRaker.com